Congressional Research Service

Reauthorizing the Secure Rural Schools and Community Self-Determination Act of 2000

Katie Hoover
Analyst in Natural Resources Policy

November 14, 2013

Congressional Research Service

7-5700

www.crs.gov

R41303

CRS Report for Congress
Prepared for Members and Committees of Congress

Summary

Many counties are compensated for the tax-exempt status of federal lands. Counties with national forest lands and with certain Bureau of Land Management (BLM) lands have historically received a percentage of agency revenues, primarily from timber sales. However, timber sales have declined substantially—by more than 90% in some areas. Thus, Congress enacted the Secure Rural Schools and Community Self-Determination Act of 2000 (SRS; P.L. 106-393) as a temporary, optional program of payments based on historic, rather than current, revenues.

Authorization for SRS payments originally expired at the end of FY2006, but through several reauthorizations the program was extended through FY2013. Congressional debates over reauthorization considered the basis and level of compensation (historical, tax equivalency, etc.); the source of funds (receipts, a new tax or revenue source, etc.); the authorized and required uses of the payments; interaction with other compensation programs (notably Payments in Lieu of Taxes); and the duration of any changes (temporary or permanent). In addition, legislation with mandatory spending, such as SRS reauthorization, raises policy questions about increasing the deficit; current budget rules to restrain deficit spending typically impose a procedural barrier to such legislation, generally requiring offsets by additional receipts or reductions in other mandatory spending.

In 2008, the Emergency Economic Stabilization Act (P.L. 110-343) enacted a four-year extension to SRS authorization through FY2011, with declining payments, a modified formula, and transition payments for certain areas. In 2012, Congress enacted a one-year extension through FY2012, and amended the program by slowing the decline in payment levels and tightening requirements that counties select a payment option promptly (P.L. 112-141). In 2013, Congress again enacted a one-year extension through FY2013 (P.L. 113-40).

Section 302 of the Budget Control Act (P.L. 112-25, as amended by P.L. 112-240) requires the President to order a sequester, or cancellation, of budgetary resources for FY2013. The sequester order took effect on March 1, 2013, and affected the SRS payment for FY2012, although BLM and Forest Service implemented the order differently from each other.

The 113th Congress has already debated many of the same issues that were debated between 2006 and 2008 and again in 2012. On October 2, 2013, the President signed P.L. 113-40 into law, reauthorizing SRS payments for FY2013. However, with the expiration of SRS at the end of FY2013, county compensation is again the subject of congressional debates. County payments are set to return to a revenue-based system for FY2014, and are likely to be significantly lower than the previous years' payments. Congress may consider extending SRS (with or without modifications), implementing other legislative proposals to address the county payments, or taking no action. No action would continue the revenue-based system that took effect upon the program's expiration. On September 20, 2013, the House passed H.R. 1526, the Restoring Healthy Forests for Healthy Communities Act, which would provide a one-time SRS payment for FY2014.

Contents

Figures

Tables

Appendixes

Contacts

Many counties are compensated for the tax-exempt status of federal lands within those counties. Counties with national forest lands and with certain Bureau of Land Management (BLM) lands have historically received a percentage of agency revenues, primarily from timber sales. However, timber sales have declined substantially since the historic high cut values in 1989—by more than 90% in some areas. Congress enacted the Secure Rural Schools and Community Self-Determination Act of 2000 (SRS, P.L. 106-393) to provide a temporary, optional system to supplant the revenue-sharing programs for the national forests, managed by the Forest Service (FS) in the Department of Agriculture, and for certain public lands administered by the BLM in the Department of the Interior.

The law authorizing these payments expired at the end of FY2006. The 109th Congress considered the program, but did not enact reauthorizing legislation. The 110th Congress extended the payments for one year through FY2007, then enacted legislation to reauthorize the program for four years with declining payments, and to modify the formula for allocating the payments. The authorization for payments was set to expire again after payments were made for FY2011, but the 112th Congress extended the program for one more year through FY2012, and amended the program by slowing the decline in payments.

The 113th Congress again enacted a one-year extension, reauthorizing the program through FY2013. The authorization is set to expire after payments are made for FY2013. Currently, payments for FY2014 will revert to a percentage of agency revenues, primarily from timber sales and recreation fees. This report explains the changes enacted for the program by the amendments in 2008 and 2012, the effect of the sequester order on the payments, and then describes the issues that Congress has debated and continues to debate in the 113th Congress.

Background

In 1908, the FS began paying 25% of its gross receipts to the states for use on roads and schools in the counties where the national forests are located; receipts come from sales, leases, rentals, or other fees for using national forest lands or resources (e.g., timber sales, recreation fees, and communication site leases).[1] This mandatory spending program was enacted to compensate local governments for the tax-exempt status of the national forests, but the compensation rate (10% of gross receipts in 1906 and 1907; 25% of gross receipts since) was not discussed in the 1906-1908 debates. This receipt-sharing program is called FS Payments to States (also referred to as the 1908 payment, or the 25% payment), because each state allocates the funds to road and school programs, although the FS determines the amount to be spent in each county based on the national forest acreage in each county. The states cannot retain any of the funds; they must be passed through to local governmental entities for use at the county level (but not necessarily to county governments) for authorized road and school programs. State law sets forth how the payments are to be allocated between road and school projects.

Congress has also enacted numerous programs to share receipts from BLM lands for various types of resource use and from various classes of land, but one program—the Oregon and California (O&C) payments—accounts for the vast majority (more than 95%) of BLM receipt-

---

[1] 16 U.S.C. §500. For more on these and other county-compensation programs with mandatory spending for federal lands, see CRS Report RL30335, *Federal Land Management Agencies' Mandatory Spending Authorities*.

sharing.[2] The O&C payments are made to the counties in western Oregon containing the revested Oregon and California grant lands returned to federal ownership for failure to fulfill the terms of the grant. The O&C counties receive 50% of the receipts from these lands. These mandatory payments go directly to the counties for any local governmental purposes. Concerns about, and proposals to alter, FS receipt-sharing payments also typically include the O&C payments, because both are substantial payments derived largely from timber receipts.

Payment History

At their pre-SRS peaks in FY1989, FS 25% payments totaled $362 million, while O&C payments totaled $110 million. FS and O&C receipts have declined substantially since FY1989, largely because of declines in timber sales (see **Figure 1**). The decline began in the Pacific Northwest,

Figure 1. Forest Service Cut Volume and Cut Value (2012 dollars)

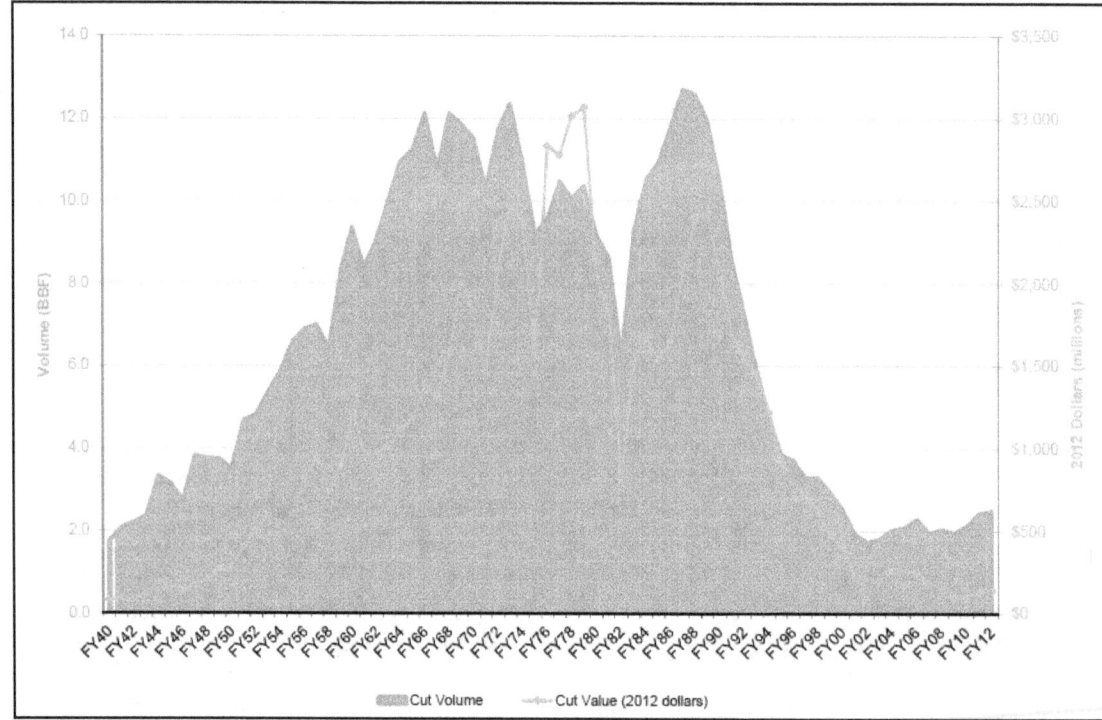

Sources: FY1977-FY2012 data: U.S. Forest Service, *Forest Cut and Sold Reports*, http://www.fs.fed.us/ forestmanagement/products/sold-harvest/cut-sold.shtml, accessed November 16, 2012. FY1940-FY1976 data: U.S. Forest Service legislative affairs office.

owing in part to efforts to protect northern spotted owl habitat and other values.[3] Provisions in the Omnibus Budget Reconciliation Act of 1993[4] directed FS payments for 17 national forests in

---

[2] For more information, see CRS Report R42951, *The Oregon & California Railroad Lands (O&C Lands): Issues for Congress.*

[3] The decline in timber harvests is attributable to a variety of factors, including a combination of forest management policies and practice, increased planning and procedural requirements, changing public preferences, economic, and industry factors.

[4] P.L. 103-66 §13982-3.

Washington, Oregon, and California and BLM payments to the O&C counties at a declining percentage (beginning at 85% in FY1994 and declining by 3 percentage points annually through FY2003) of the average payments for FY1986-FY1990. Declining federal timber sales in other regions led to the nationwide SRS program replacing these safety net or "owl" payments in 2000.

Similar to the owl payments for the Pacific Northwest, the SRS program was an optional payment counties could elect to receive instead of receiving the 25% receipt-sharing payment. As originally enacted, the SRS payment was calculated as an average of the three highest payments between FY1986 and FY1999. With the extension in FY2007, the SRS payment calculation was modified to also consider county population and per capita income.

Payments under SRS are substantial, and significantly greater than the receipt-sharing payments would be. For example, the average annual total SRS payment for FY2001 through FY2011 was $383 million. In contrast, under the receipt-sharing system prior to the enactment of SRS, the average annual total payment was $273 million from FY1990 through FY2000. **Figure 2** shows a comparison of the FS actual payments to estimates of what the payments would have been had

Figure 2. FS Total Payments and Estimated Payments

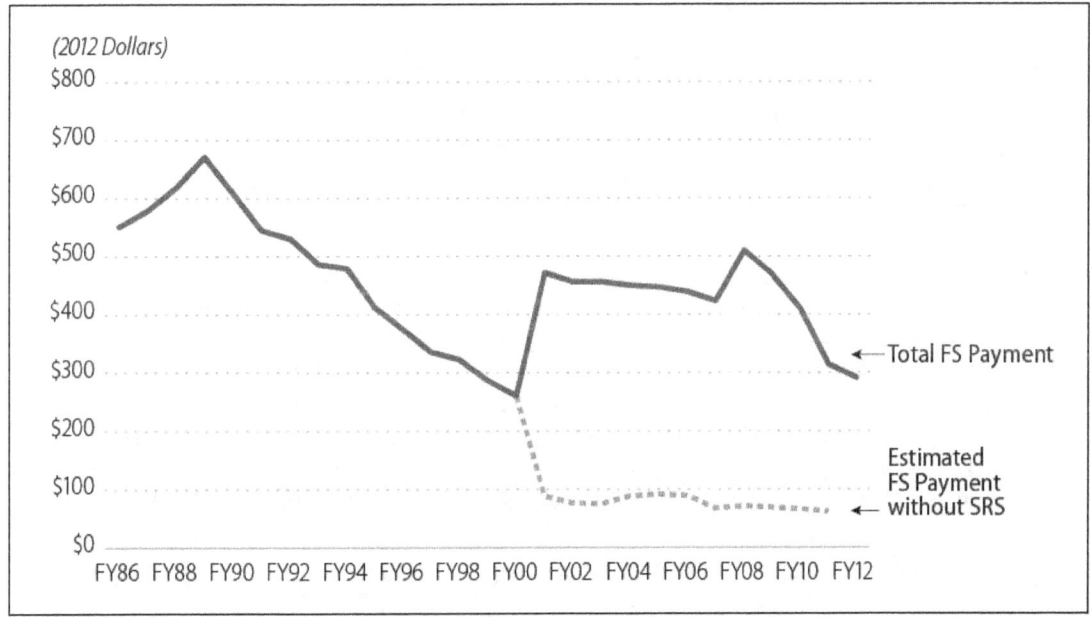

Source: CRS. FS total payments are from the annual Forest Service report, *All Service Receipts: Final Payment Summary Report PNF (ASR-10-01)*, available from http://www.fs.usda.gov/main/pts/home. The estimated FS payments if SRS had not been enacted for FY2001-FY2007 are from an unpublished spreadsheet received from Rick Alexander, Secure Rural Schools Act National Program Manager, U.S. Forest Service, on November 30, 2011. The estimated payments for FY2008-FY2011 are from an FS spreadsheet available at http://www.fs.usda.gov/main/pts/home.

Notes: The data presented includes payments under the 25% Payments to States and SRS Title I and Title III programs, but does not include SRS Title II payments and miscellaneous county payments authorized through various other FS payment programs not discussed in this report, such as payments from land utilization projects.

SRS not been enacted. FS receipts (for receipt-sharing purposes) in FY2011 totaled $323 million.[5] If receipt-sharing had been used rather than SRS payments then the 25% payments would have been less than $80 million. However, FY2011 payments under SRS actually totaled $308 million. Similarly, BLM timber receipts from western Oregon (which includes some non-O&C lands) totaled $22 million in FY2011.[6] If 50% payments had been used, then $11 million would have been transferred to the counties, compared to SRS payments of $40 million in FY2011. If SRS is not reauthorized, FY2014 payments will again be based on a percentage of agency receipts.

Relationship with Other Federal Compensation Programs

In addition to these receipt-sharing programs, Congress enacted the Payments in Lieu of Taxes (PILT) Program.[7] PILT payments to counties are based on "eligible" federal lands, including national forests and O&C lands, in each county (but are restricted in counties with very low populations). PILT payments are reduced (to a minimum payment per acre) by other payment programs—including FS Payments to States and BLM's O&C payments—so changes to these latter programs may also affect a county's payments under PILT. This also explains why FY2012 PILT payments to Colorado were double the PILT payments to Oregon, even though there is more federal land in Oregon (32.6 million acres) than in Colorado (23.8 million acres).

As enacted, PILT requires annual appropriations. If the appropriations are less than the authorized total payments, each county gets its calculated pro rata share of the appropriations. However, the 2008 and 2012 SRS amendments also made PILT payments mandatory spending for FY2008-FY2012. Thus, for those fiscal years, each county received 100% of its authorized PILT payment.

Geographic Distribution of SRS and PILT Payments

An issue of concern to Congress is the geographic allocation of the SRS and PILT payments. **Table 1** shows the payments for FY2012. The only O&C payment is made to Oregon, and Oregon also receives the largest FS payment. With the O&C payment of approximately $63 million, Oregon received nearly 35% of the total payments made in FY2012. The next-largest payments are in California, which received just over 10% of the total payments. PILT payments are more evenly distributed, with no state receiving more than 10% of the total payments.

Table 1. FY2012 FS and PILT Payments, by State

(in thousands of dollars)

	FS	PILT		FS	PILT
Alabama	$1,844.2	$805.2	Nebraska	$196.8	$1,131.4
Alaska	$13,878.3	$26,894.5	Nevada	$3,630.3	$23,917.8
Arizona	$13,080.4	$32,886.6	New Hampshire	$546.7	$1,800.9

---

[5] Data provided by the Forest Service Legislative Affairs office, February 21, 2013.

[6] U.S. Dept. of the Interior, Bureau of Land Management, *Public Land Statistics, 2011*, Table 3-12, http://www.blm.gov/public_land_statistics/pls11/pls2011.pdf.

[7] See CRS Report RL31392, *PILT (Payments in Lieu of Taxes): Somewhat Simplified.*

	FS	PILT		FS	PILT
Arkansas	$6,653.1	$5,277.0	New Jersey	$0.0	$99.4
California	$35,777.1	$40,272.0	New Mexico	$10,264.3	$34,917.8
Colorado	$13,053.1	$27,724.6	New York	$18.8	$152.3
Connecticut	$0.0	$29.6	North Carolina	$1,902.5	$4,030.5
Delaware	$0.0	$18.3	North Dakota	$0.6	$1,418.4
Florida	$2,340.7	$4,891.7	Ohio	$268.4	$521.9
Georgia	$1,549.6	$2,242.6	Oklahoma	$916.7	$2,740.2
Hawaii	$0.0	$335.0	Oregon	$63,015.5	$14,005.0
Idaho	$26,628.3	$26,560.2	Pennsylvania	$3,330.6	$610.8
Illinois	$253.9	$1,140.8	Rhode Island	$0.0	$0.0
Indiana	$269.0	$465.8	South Carolina	$1,772.3	$406.0
Iowa	$0.0	$466.9	South Dakota	$1,600.5	$5,363.8
Kansas	$0.0	$1,131.4	Tennessee	$1,149.6	$1,826.5
Kentucky	$1,586.5	$1,835.8	Texas	$2,331.1	$4,644.6
Louisiana	$1,734.5	$610.0	Utah	$10,579.8	$36,038.6
Maine	$71.5	$316.0	Vermont	$334.1	$942.2
Maryland	$0.0	$102.4	Virginia	$1,625.1	$3,113.1
Massachusetts	$0.0	$114.4	Washington	$20,094.8	$15,340.0
Michigan	$3,826.0	$4,150.5	West Virginia	$1,788.6	$2,953.2
Minnesota	$8,477.5	$1,944.1	Wisconsin	$1,903.0	$1,087.2
Mississippi	$5,552.0	$2,736.8	Wyoming	$4,309.9	$25,315.3
Missouri	$3,352.7	$2,7346.8	Other[a]	$147.2	$63.9
Montana	$19,746.9	$26,152.0	**Total**	**$255,356.3**	**$381,647.9**

Sources: FS: U.S. Dept. of Agriculture, Forest Service, "All Service Receipts (ASR), Final Payment Summary Report PNF (ASR-10-01)," http://www.fs.usda.gov/Internet/FSE_DOCUMENTS/stelprdb5407120.pdf. **O&C:** U.S. Dept. of the Interior, Bureau of Land Management, *FY2012 Secure Rural Schools Act Payments*, http://www.blm.gov/or/rac/files/rac-payments.pdf. **PILT:** U.S. Dept. of the Interior, *Payments in Lieu of Taxes (PILT) Payments by State*, http://www.doi.gov/pilt/state-payments.cfm?fiscal_yr=2012.

a.   "Other" includes the District of Columbia, Guam, Puerto Rico, and the Virgin Islands.

Receipt-Sharing Program Concerns and Responses

SRS was enacted as a temporary, optional payment program based on historic revenues rather than a program based on sharing a percentage of current receipts. Congress, the affected counties, and other observers have raised three concerns about FS and O&C receipt-sharing programs.[8] The primary focus has been on the decline in FS and O&C receipts due to the decline in timber sales,

---

[8] Forest Counties Payments Committee, *Recommendations for Making Payments to States and Counties: Report to Congress* (Washington: GPO, 2003). The committee was established in §320 of the FY2001 Interior and Related Agencies Appropriations Act, P.L. 106-291.

but the annual uncertainty about payment amounts and the linkage between timber revenue and county revenue are also concerns.

Declining Timber Receipts

A primary concern about the receipt-sharing programs is how counties are responding to declining revenue. National forest receipts (subject to sharing) declined from their peak of $1.53 billion in FY1989 to $266 million in FY2003—a drop of 83% from the FY1989 level (**Figure 1**). Estimated receipts for FY2012 were $340 million. In some areas, the decline was even greater; for example, payments to the eastern Oregon counties containing the Ochoco National Forest fell from $10 million in FY1991 to $309,000 in FY1998—a decline of 97% in seven years. The impact of these declining revenues to individual counties is varied, ranging from minimal to substantial. Some counties in Oregon, for example, have begun exploring alternative options to generating revenue to replace the loss of timber receipts and declining SRS payments.[9]

Annually Fluctuating Payments

Another concern has been annual fluctuations in the payments based on revenue generated. Even in areas with modest declines or increases, the payments varied widely from year to year. From FY1985 to FY2000, the payments from each national forest had fluctuations of an *average* of nearly 30% annually—that is, on average, a county's payment in any year was likely to be nearly 30% higher or lower than its payment the preceding year. Such wide annual fluctuations imposed serious budgeting difficulties on the counties.

Linkage

A third, longer-term concern is referred to as *linkage*. Some observers have noted that, because the counties receive a portion of receipts, they are rewarded for advocating receipt-generating activities (principally timber sales) and for opposing management that might reduce or constrain such activities (e.g., designating wilderness areas or protecting commercial, tribal, or sport fish harvests). County governments have thus often been allied with the timber industry, and sometimes opposed to environmental and other interest groups, in debates over FS management and budget decisions. This source of funds was deemed appropriate when the FS program was created (albeit, prior to creation of federal income taxes). Some interests support retaining the linkage between county compensation and agency receipts; local support for receipt-generating activities is seen as appropriate by these constituencies, because such activities usually also provide local employment and income, especially in rural areas where unemployment is often high. Others assert that ending the linkage is important so that local government officials can be independent in supporting whatever management decisions benefit their locality, rather than having financial incentives to support particular decisions.

---

[9] See http://www.seattlepi.com/news/science/article/Curry-County-Ore-rejecting-public-safety-tax-4955794.php.

Historical Proposals to Change the Receipt-Sharing System

Concerns about the FS and BLM programs have led to various proposals over the years to alter the compensation system. Most have focused on some form of *tax equivalency*—compensating the states and counties at roughly the same level as if the lands were privately owned and managed. Many acknowledge the validity of this approach for fairly and consistently compensating state and county governments. However, most also note the difficulty in developing a tax equivalency compensation system, because counties and states use a wide variety of mechanisms to tax individuals and corporations—property taxes, sales taxes, income taxes, excise taxes, severance taxes, and more. Thus, developing a single federal compensation system for the tax-exempt status of federal lands may be very difficult if not impossible.

In his 1984 budget request, President Reagan proposed replacing the receipt-sharing programs with a tax equivalency system, with a guaranteed minimum payment. The counties argued that the proposal was clearly intended to reduce payments, noting that the budget request projected savings of $40.5 million (12%) under the proposal. The change was not enacted. The FY1986 FS budget request included a proposal to change the payments to 25% of *net* receipts (after deducting administrative costs). Legislation to effect this change was not offered.

In 1993, President Clinton proposed a 10-year payment program to offset the decline in FS and O&C timber sales, and thus payments, resulting from efforts to protect northern spotted owls and other values in the Pacific Northwest. Congress enacted this program in Section 13982 of the 1993 Omnibus Budget Reconciliation Act (P.L. 103-66). These "spotted owl" payments began in 1994 at 85% of the FY1986-FY1990 average payments, declining by 3 percentage points annually, to 58% in 2003, but with payments after FY1999 at the higher of either this formula or the standard payment.

In his FY1999 budget request, President Clinton announced that he would propose legislation "to stabilize the payments" by extending the spotted owl payments formula to all national forests. The proposal would have directed annual payments from "any funds in the Treasury not otherwise appropriated," at the higher of (1) the FY1997 payment, or (2) 76% of the FY1986-FY1990 average payment. This approach would have increased payments in areas with large payment declines while decreasing payments in other areas, as well as eliminating annual fluctuations in payments and de-linking the payments from receipts. The Administration's proposed legislation was not introduced in Congress. The FY2000 and FY2001 FS budget requests contained similar programs, but no legislative proposals were offered.

The National Association of Counties (NACo) proposed an alternative in 1999.[10] The NACo proposal would have provided the counties with the higher of (1) the standard payment, or (2) a replacement payment determined by the three highest consecutive annual payments for each county between FY1986 and FY1995, indexed for inflation. NACo also proposed "a long-term solution ... to allow for the appropriate, sustainable, and environmentally sensitive removal of timber from the National Forests" by establishing local advisory councils. The NACo approach would have maintained or increased the payments and might have reduced the annual fluctuations, but would likely have retained the linkage between receipts and payments in at least some areas.

---

[10] National Association of Counties, *NACo Resolution in Support of a Forest Counties "Safety Net,"* Washington, DC, April 21, 1999.

Legislative History of the Secure Rural Schools and Community Self-Determination Act of 2000, as Amended

Several bills were introduced in the 106th Congress to alter FS and O&C payments. After extensive debates, Congress enacted the Secure Rural Schools and Community Self-Determination Act of 2000 (SRS, P.L. 106-393). The act established an alternative payment system for FY2001-FY2006. At each county's discretion, the states with FS land and counties with O&C land received either the regular receipt-sharing payments or 100% of the average of the three highest payments between FY1986 and FY1999. Title I of the act directed that counties receiving less than $100,000 under the alternative system could distribute the entire payment to roads and schools in the same manner as the 25% payments. However, counties receiving at least $100,000 under the alternative system were required to spend 15%-20% of the payment on (1) federal land projects proposed by local resource advisory committees and approved by the appropriate Secretary if the projects met specified criteria, including compliance with all applicable laws and regulations and with resource management and other plans (identified in Title II of the act) or (2) certain county programs (specified in Title III of the act). Funds needed to achieve the full payment were permanently appropriated, and came first from agency receipts (excluding deposits to special accounts and trust funds) and then from "any funds in the Treasury not otherwise appropriated."

With the enactment of SRS, the FS total payment to counties rose from $194 million in FY2000 (in nominal dollars) to $346 million in FY2001 (**Figure 2**). For the initial six years SRS was authorized, the average FS payment was $360 million annually, more than $130 million above the average annual FS payment for the six years prior to the enactment of SRS (FY1995-FY2000).

Reauthorization Efforts in the 110th Congress

SRS expired at the end of FY2006, with final payments made at the end of December 2006. Legislation to extend the program was considered in the 110th Congress; various bills would have extended the program for one or seven years, and one specified funding it with a miniscule (0.00086%) rescission of "any [FY2007] non-defense discretionary account." An amendment to the FY2007 continuing resolution (H.R. 2) to extend the program for one year was offered and then withdrawn.

The debate continued in the Emergency Supplemental Appropriations Act for FY2007 (H.R. 1591, the U.S. Troop Readiness, Veterans' Care, Katrina Recovery, and Iraq Accountability Appropriations Act, 2007). The House included a one-year extension of the program. The Senate amended the bill (S.Amdt. 709) to extend the program for five years (FY2008-FY2012) and significantly change the formula for allocating funds to the counties; the change was to address the concentration of payments in certain areas by spreading payments more broadly (as discussed below). The conference agreed to the House-passed version (a one-year extension), but the bill was vetoed by President George W. Bush.

A new version of Emergency Supplemental Appropriations for FY2007 (H.R. 2206) was introduced on May 8, 2007. This bill also included a one-year extension of SRS payments, and it was signed into law as P.L. 110-28 on May 25, 2007. Title V, Chapter 4, Section 5401, authorized payments of $100.0 million from receipts and of $425.0 million from appropriations, to "be made, to the maximum extent practicable, in the same amounts, for the same purposes, and in the same manner as were made to States and counties in 2006 under that Act." Thus, preliminary FY2007 payments were made at the end of September 2007, with final payments made at the end of December 2007.

Another bill—the Public Land Communities Transition Assistance Act (H.R. 3058)—was introduced in July 2007 to extend, modify, and phase out the SRS payments; it was similar to the 2007 Senate Amendment to H.R. 1591. The House Natural Resources Committee held a subcommittee hearing on the bill on July 26, 2007, and a committee markup on September 26, 2007. The committee ordered the bill reported, amended, by voice vote. The bill was brought up on the House floor under suspension of the rules procedures, but did not garner the two-thirds vote needed to pass under this procedure, and it was not brought up later under other procedures.

Four-Year Extension through FY2011 Enacted in the 110th Congress

On October 1, 2008, the Senate passed H.R. 1424, the Emergency Economic Stabilization Act, with a provision similar to the 2007 Senate Amendment to H.R. 1591 in Section 601 (in Title VI—Other Provisions, Division C—Tax Extenders and Alternative Minimum Tax Relief). The House agreed to the Senate amendments on October 3, 2008, and President George W. Bush signed P.L. 110-343 into law.

Section 601(a) of H.R. 1424 extended the SRS payment program with several changes: "full funding" that declines over four years; the basis for calculating payments; transition payments for certain states; and the use of SRS funds for Title II and Title III activities. In addition, Section 601(b) modified the original FS 25% payment program (under which counties can get compensation in lieu of SRS payments and for payments after SRS expires). Finally, Section 601(c) provided five years of mandatory spending for the PILT program.

Full Funding

The act defined *full funding* for SRS in Section 3(11). For FY2008, full funding was $500 million; for FY2009-FY2011, full funding was 90% of the previous year's funding. However, total payments exceeded the full funding amount in the first two years; payments under SRS totaled $572.9 million in FY2008 and $612.8 million in FY2009. This occurred because the *calculated payments* (discussed below) are based on full funding, as defined in the bill, but the act also authorized *transition payments* (discussed below) in lieu of the calculated payments in eight states. Since the transition payments exceeded the calculated payments for those states, the total payments were higher than the full funding amount.

Calculated Payments

SRS payments to each state (for FS lands) or county (for O&C lands) differed significantly from the payments made under the original SRS; **Table A-1** shows the dollars and share of total SRS payments in each state in FY2006 and FY2009. Payments under Section 102 were based on historic revenue-sharing payments (like SRS), but modified based on each county's share of federal land and relative income level. The payment calculations required a multiple-step process:

- **Step 1.** Determine the three highest revenue-sharing payments between FY1986 and FY1999 for each eligible county, and calculate the average of the three.[11]

- **Step 2.** Calculate the proportion of these payments in each county (divide each county's three-highest average [**Step 1**] by the total of three-highest average in all eligible counties, with separate calculations for FS lands and O&C lands).

- **Step 3.** Calculate the proportion of FS and O&C lands in each eligible county (divide each county's FS and O&C acreage by the total FS and O&C acreage in all eligible counties, with separate calculations for FS lands and O&C lands).

- **Step 4.** Average these two proportions (add the payment proportion [**Step 2**] and the acreage proportion [**Step 3**] and divide by 2, with separate calculations for FS lands and O&C lands). This is the *base share* for counties with FS lands and the *50% base share* for counties with O&C lands.

- **Step 5.** Calculate each county's *income adjustment* by dividing the per capita personal income in each county by the median per capita personal income in all eligible counties.

- **Step 6.** Adjust each county's base share [**Step 4**] by its relative income (divide each county's base share or 50% base share by its income adjustment [**Step 5**]).

- **Step 7.** Calculate each county's *adjusted share* or *50% adjusted share* as the county's proportion of its base share adjusted by its relative income [**Step 6**] from the total adjusted shares in all eligible counties (divide each county's result from **Step 6** by the total for all eligible counties [FS and O&C combined]).

In essence, the amendment differed from the original SRS by basing half the payments on historic revenues and half on proportion of FS and O&C land, with an adjustment based on relative county income. This was done because of the concentration of payments under the original SRS to Oregon, Washington, and California (more than 75% of payments in FY2006; see **Table A-1**). Several counties opted out of the amended SRS system, while others opted in, because of the altered allocation. For example, in FY2006 100% of the payments to Pennsylvania were under SRS, but in FY2009 only 54% of the payments to Pennsylvania were under SRS. Conversely, in FY2006 none of the payments to New Hampshire were under SRS, but in FY2009, 44% of the payments to New Hampshire were under SRS.

In addition, the act set a full payment amount allocated among all counties that chose to participate in the program (eligible counties). Thus, the fewer counties that participated (i.e., the more that opted for the original payment programs), the more each participating county received.

Transition Payments

In lieu of the calculated payments under Section 102, the counties in eight states—California, Louisiana, Oregon, Pennsylvania, South Carolina, South Dakota, Texas, and Washington—received transition payments for three fiscal years, FY2008-FY2010. These counties were included in the calculations, but received payments of a fixed percentage of the FY2006 payments under SRS, instead of their calculated payments. The schedule in the act specified

---

[11] Eligible counties are those that choose to receive payments under this program; counties that choose to continue to receive payments under the original revenue-sharing programs are excluded from these calculations.

FY2008 payments equaling 90% of FY2006 payments, FY2009 payments at 81% of FY2006 payments, and FY2010 payments at 73% of FY2006 payments. Because the transition payments were higher than the calculated payments (using the multi-step formula, above), total payments have been greater than the "full funding" defined in the act.

Title II and Title III Activities

As with the original SRS, the amended version allowed counties with less than $100,000 in annual payments to use 100% of the payments for roads and schools (or any governmental purpose for O&C counties). However, it modified the requirement that counties with "modest distributions" (annual payments of more than $100,000 but less than $350,000) use 15%-20% of the funds for Title II projects (reinvestment in federal lands). Instead, these counties could use the required 15%-20% either for Title II projects or for Title III projects (county projects). Counties with payments of more than $350,000 were limited to 7% of the payments for Title III programs. The amendment also modified the authorized uses of Title III funds, deleting some authorized uses (e.g., community work centers) while expanding authorized uses related to community wildfire protection.

Income Averaging

The extension also altered the FS 25% Payment to States program. It changed the payment from 25% of current-year gross receipts to 25% of average gross receipts over the past seven years— essentially a seven-year rolling average of receipts. This reduced the annual fluctuation in payments, providing more stability in the annual payments. Thus payments increase more slowly than in the past when and where national forest receipts are rising, but decline more slowly when and where receipts are falling. This change immediately affected counties with FS land that chose not to participate in the SRS payment program, and will affect all counties with FS land in FY2013 (unless SRS is reauthorized or some other alternative is enacted).

Payments in Lieu of Taxes (PILT)

Section 601(c) of the act provided mandatory spending for the PILT program for five years, FY2008-FY2012. This meant that eligible counties received the full calculated PILT payment for those five years—a significant increase in PILT payments, since appropriations averaged less than two-thirds of the calculated payments over the past decade. After FY2012, PILT would again require annual appropriations, unless Congress extends mandatory spending for the program.

One-Year Extension through FY2012 Enacted in the 112th Congress

SRS was set to expire at the end of FY2011, with final payments made at the end of December 2011. Legislation to extend the program for five years was considered in the 112th Congress. The County Payments Reauthorization Act of 2011 (S. 1692 and H.R. 3599) would have extended SRS through 2016 and included provisions to slow the decline of the full funding levels to 95% of the preceding fiscal year. Neither the Senate nor the House version was reported out of committee.

On April 24, 2012, the Senate passed S. 1813, the Moving Ahead for Progress in the 21st Century Act (MAP-21), with a one-year extension for SRS. The companion legislation in the House did not contain the extension, but the House agreed to the Senate amendments on June 29, 2012. On July 6, 2012, President Obama signed P.L. 112-141 into law.

Section 100101 of P.L. 112-141 extended the SRS program through FY2012 with funding at 95% of the FY2011 level, and included requirements for the counties to select their payment option in a timely manner. The program expired on September 30, 2012, meaning that payments will revert to the original 25% receipt-sharing formula for FY2013 (or the 50% receipt-sharing formula for the O&C lands), absent further action by Congress.

One-Year Extension through FY2013 Enacted in the 113th Congress

SRS was again set to expire at the end of FY2012, with final payments made by February 2013. Legislation to extend the program for one year was enacted in the 113th Congress. On September 19, 2013, the Senate Committee on Energy and Natural Resources reported S. 783, the Helium Stewardship Act of 2013, which included a one-year extension of SRS through FY2013. The House had already passed its version of the Helium Stewardship Act of 2013, H.R. 527, on April 26, 2013. The Senate amended and passed H.R. 527 on September 19, 2013, which included the SRS extension. On September 26, 2013, both chambers had resolved the differences in the bill and passed the legislation, reauthorizing SRS for FY2013 at 95% of the FY2012 SRS payment. President Obama signed the bill into law on October 2, 2013 (P.L. 113-40).

Legislative Activity in the 113th Congress

In the first session, the 113th Congress reauthorized SRS for FY2013 and has held hearings to discuss options for modifying the payment program. On March 19, 2013, the Senate Energy and Natural Resources Committee held a hearing to discuss options for reauthorizing and reforming SRS and PILT.[12] SRS and county payment programs were also discussed in several House legislative hearings.

The 113th Congress is also conducting oversight on the SRS program. On November 5, 2013, Chairman Hastings announced, in letters sent to both the Secretary of Agriculture and the Director of OMB, the potential for an oversight hearing, tentatively planned for November 20, 2013, on the decision to sequester the FY2012 SRS payment.[13]

The President's FY2014 budget request for the Forest Service and the BLM proposes a five-year reauthorization of SRS, with mandatory funding, starting at $278 million for FY2014 and declining to $106 million by FY2017.[14] The President's proposal also includes decreasing the Title I and Title III allocation while increasing the Title II allocation.

---

[12] U.S. Congress, Senate Energy and Natural Resources, *Keeping the Commitment to Rural Communities*, 113th Cong., 1 sess., March 19, 2013, pp. http://www.energy.senate.gov/public/index.cfm/2013/3/full-committee-hearing-funding-programs-for-rural-communities.

[13] House Natural Resources Committee, press release, November 5, 2013, http://naturalresources.house.gov/news/documentsingle.aspx?DocumentID=360388.

[14] U.S. Forest Service, *FY2014 Budget Justification*, pp. 12-58, http://www fs fed.us/aboutus/budget/.

FY2014 Reauthorization Efforts

SRS is set to expire after the FY2013 payments are made in FY2014. The 113th Congress is now considering options for reauthorizing or modifying SRS for FY2014. On September 20, 2013, the House passed H.R. 1526, the Restoring Healthy Forests for Healthy Communities Act. Section 501 of H.R. 1526 would direct the FS and BLM to distribute a payment to eligible counties in February 2015, essentially a FY2014 SRS payment. The payment amount would be equal to the FY2010 payment for the counties receiving Forest Service payments. For the O&C counties, the payment amount would be $27 million less than the FY2010 payment. After that payment is made, county payments would return to a revenue-sharing system. H.R. 1526 would establish Forest Resource Revenue Areas within at least half of the National Forest System, and create a fiduciary responsibility to generate revenue by removing forest products for the beneficiary counties (Section 103(d)). In Section 502, H.R. 1526 would change the calculation formula for the FS 25% Payment to States program. It would change the payment from 25% of average gross receipts over the past seven years to 25% of current-year gross receipts.

Sequestration Issues

Section 302 of the Budget Control Act (BCA; P.L. 112-25, as amended by P.L. 112-240) required the President to order a sequester, or cancellation, of budgetary resources for FY2013, in the event that Congress did not enact deficit reduction of at least $1.2 trillion by January 15, 2012.[15] Congress did not enact such deficit reduction by that date, and on March 1, 2013, the Office of Management and Budget (OMB) determined the amount of the total sequestration for FY2013 to be approximately $85 billion.[16]

Under the BCA, half of the total reduction calculated pursuant to paragraph (3) for FY2013 is allocated to defense spending, and the other half to non-defense spending.[17] Within each half, the reductions are further allocated between discretionary appropriations and direct spending.[18] Discretionary appropriations are defined in the BCA as budgetary resources provided in annual appropriations acts.[19] In contrast, direct spending is defined to include budget authority provided by law other than appropriations acts.[20] The BCA further requires OMB to calculate a uniform percentage reduction that is to be applied to each program, project, or activity within the direct spending category.[21] For the direct spending category, OMB has determined this percentage to be 5.1% for FY2013.

---

[15] 2 U.S.C. §901A. The sequester was originally supposed to be ordered on January 2, 2013, but was delayed by the American Taxpayer Relief Act of 2012, P.L. 112-240, until March 1, 2013. For more information on sequestration issues, see CRS Report R42972, *Sequestration as a Budget Enforcement Process: Frequently Asked Questions.*

[16] This amount was identified based on a formula set forth in §302 of the BCA.

[17] 2 U.S.C. §901A(4).

[18] 2 U.S.C. §901A(6).

[19] 2 U.S.C. §900(7).

[20] 2 U.S.C. §900(8). Budget authority is further defined as "the authority provided by Federal law to incur financial obligations." 2 U.S.C. §622.

[21] Although not relevant here, additional restrictions are placed on the degree by which Medicare payments in the direct spending category may be reduced. 2 U.S.C. §901a(8).

Section 102(d)(3)(e) of SRS directs that payments for a fiscal year are to be made to the state as soon as practicable after the end of that fiscal year, meaning that the FY2012 payment is made in FY2013.[22] Because the authority to make these payments is not provided in an annual appropriations act, such payments are not discretionary spending for purposes of the BCA. These payments are classified as non-defense, *direct* spending for purposes of sequestration, as direct spending is defined to include all budget authority provided in law other than annual appropriations acts.[23] The BCA exempts a number of programs from sequestration; however, the payments under SRS do not appear to be identified as exempt.[24] Consequently, these payments would appear to be subject to sequestration as non-defense, direct spending.

BLM Sequestration of SRS Funds

BLM issues SRS payments only for the O&C lands in Oregon. In February 2013, BLM distributed $36 million to the 18 O&C counties in Oregon for FY2012 SRS payments. However, DOI held back 10% of the scheduled payments across all three titles in anticipation of the possibility of sequestration. The reduction to DOI's SRS program required by sequestration was 5.1% of the total payment, or $2.0 million.[25] Since the sequestered amount was less than the amount withheld, DOI-BLM owed an additional SRS payment for the difference. In May 2013, BLM distributed the remaining 4.9% of the payment, resulting in a total $38 million SRS payment to the O&C counties for FY2012.[26]

Forest Service Sequestration of SRS Funds

The Forest Service distributed the full FY2012 SRS payments in January and February 2013, without withholding any amount in preparation for the potential sequester order. On March 19, 2013, the Forest Service announced it would seek to recover from the states the 5.1% of the payments that were subject to sequestration.[27] In letters sent to each affected governor, the Forest Service outlined two repayment options and asked for the states to respond by April 19, 2013, with how they planned to repay. Invoices for repayment were not included. In addition to repaying the 5.1%, the FS offered the states the option of having the full sequestered amount taken out of Title II funds (for those states with enough Title II money). Three states—Alaska, Washington, and Wyoming—have publicly indicated their intention to not repay the SRS funds.[28] In an April 16, 2013, hearing before the Senate Committee on Energy and Natural Resources, the FS indicated that invoices for the repayment would be sent in late April 2013.

On August 5, 2013, the Forest Service sent additional letters which included invoices for the repayment to the governors of the 18 states with insufficient Title II money to cover the

---

[22] 16 U.S.C. §7112(e).

[23] 2 U.S.C. §900(8).

[24] 2 U.S.C. §905.

[25] Testimony of DOI Deputy Assistant Secretary Pamela K. Haze, in U.S. Congress, Senate Committee on Energy and Natural Resources, *Keeping the Commitment to Rural Communities,* hearing, 113th Cong., 1st sess., March 19, 2013.

[26] Personal communication with BLM Legislative Affairs office, June 19, 2013.

[27] Testimony of Forest Service Chief Thomas Tidwell, in U.S. Congress, Senate Committee on Energy and Natural Resources, *Keeping the Commitment to Rural Communities,* hearing, 113th Cong., 1st sess., March 19, 2013. SRS payments are made from the Forest Service to the states, which then distribute the payment to the eligible counties.

[28] Phil Taylor, "Hastings probes Forest Service's withholding of timber payments," *E&E News,* May 21, 2013.

sequestered amount.[29] The invoices outline three options for the affected states to take within 30 days: pay the debt in full; agree to a payment plan; or petition for administrative review of the debt. The invoices also included a Notice of Indebtedness to the U.S. Forest Service and Intent to Collect by Administrative Offset, which describes the basis of the indebtedness and the Forest Service's intent to offset future payments—without assessing penalties—from future Forest Service and Department of Agriculture state payments. As of November 13, 2013, one state has responded to the invoice and remitted an SRS sequester-related payment—New Hampshire paid $27,884.17—and no collection efforts have been initiated by the Forest Service or Treasury Department.[30]

On August 20, 2013, the Forest Service sent additional letters to the governors of the 22 states that had sufficient Title II money to cover the sequestered amount.[31] The letters informed the governors that the Title II allocations are being reduced by the sequestered amount.

On September 4, 2013, House Natural Resources Committee Chairman Doc Hastings issued subpoenas to the Secretary of Agriculture and the Director of OMB seeking documents related to the decision to sequester the SRS payment by September 18, 2013.[32] On November 5, 2013, Chairman Hastings sent another letter to both the Secretary of Agriculture and the Director of OMB indicating their failure to fully comply with the subpoenas and announced a planned oversight hearing on the issue, tentatively planned for November 20, 2013.[33]

Legislative Issues

Congress may consider extending SRS, with or without modifications, implementing other legislative proposals to address the county payments, or taking no action (thus continuing the revenue-based system that took effect upon the program's expiration). Generally, six issues commonly have been raised about compensating counties for the tax-exempt status of federal lands: the lands covered; the basis for compensation; the source of funds; the authorized and required uses of the payments; interaction with other compensation programs; and the duration of the new system. In addition, any new mandatory spending in excess of the baseline that would result in an increase in the deficit may be subject to budget rules, such as congressional pay-as-you-go (PAYGO) rules, which generally require budgetary offsets.[34]

---

[29] The following states did not have sufficient Title II funds to cover the sequester and received invoices: AL, AR, GA, IL, IN, ME, MN, MO, NC, ND, NE, NH, NY, OH, PA, PR, TN, VT, and VA. WA received a letter and invoice to collect money from a special act payment, but the letter also indicated the total SRS Title II reduction.

[30] WA paid $317.15 to reimburse for the sequester-related overpayment of a special act payment. Personal communication with Katherine Armstrong, Legislative Affairs Specialist, Forest Service, November 13, 2013.

[31] The following states had the sequester withheld entirely from their Title II funds: AK, AZ, CA, CO, FL, ID, KY, LA, MI, MS, MT, NM, NV, OK, OR, SC, SD, TX, UT, WI, WV, and WY.

[32] House Natural Resources Committee, Press Release September 4, 2013, http://naturalresources house.gov/news/documentsingle.aspx?DocumentID=347606.

[33] House Natural Resources Committee, Press Release November 5, 2013, http://naturalresources house.gov/news/documentsingle.aspx?DocumentID=360388.

[34] For an overview of federal budget procedures, see CRS Report 98-721, *Introduction to the Federal Budget Process*. For background on PAYGO rules, see CRS Report RL34300, *Pay-As-You-Go Procedures for Budget Enforcement*.

Offsets for New Mandatory Spending

One policy issue concerns legislation with mandatory spending that would increase federal expenditures, and whether such spending should be offset so as not to increase the deficit. Congress has enacted a set of budget rules requiring that most legislation that creates new or extends existing mandatory spending (in excess of the baseline) be balanced—offset—by increases in receipts or decreases in other mandatory spending. The budget rules may be waived or set aside in particular instances, but the increased deficit spending remains a consideration.

Legislation to reauthorize the Secure Rural Schools and Community Self-Determination Act of 2000 (with or without other modifications), or to enact a different alternative, would require an offset—increased revenues or decreased spending from other mandatory spending accounts—or a waiver to the budget rules. In 2000, Congress provided such a waiver by including a specific type of provision, called a reserve fund, in the budget resolution.

In 2006, to fund a six-year reauthorization of SRS, the Bush Administration proposed selling some federal lands. To fund the O&C payments, the BLM would have accelerated its land sales under Section 203 of the Federal Land Policy and Management Act of 1976 (FLPMA; 43 U.S.C. §1713). For the FS payments, estimated at $800 million, the FS would have sold approximately 300,000 acres of national forest land. This would have required legislation, as the FS currently has only very narrow authority to sell any lands. The Administration offered draft legislation to authorize these land sales, but no bill to authorize that level of national forest land sales was introduced in the 109th Congress. Instead, Congress again included a reserve fund for SRS payments in the budget resolution.

In 2007, the Bush Administration again proposed selling national forest lands to fund a phase-out of SRS payments, with half of the land sale revenues to be used for other programs (including land acquisition and conservation education). Again, no legislation to authorize national forest land sales was introduced.

Lands Covered

SRS includes payments only for national forests and for the O&C lands. Some observers have noted that these compensation programs provide substantial funding for the specified lands, while other federal lands that are exempt from state and local taxation receive little or nothing. The easiest comparison is with the national grasslands. Some have questioned the logic of compensating national forest counties with 25% of gross receipts and protecting these counties from declines in receipts under SRS, while compensating national grassland counties with 25% of net receipts and excluding them from SRS. Both forests and grasslands are part of the National Forest System, although the laws authorizing their establishment differ.

More significantly, many other tax-exempt federal lands provide little compensation to local governments. The BLM has numerous compensation programs, but generally the payments are quite small. (The O&C payments account for about 95% of BLM compensation payments, but O&C lands are only about 1% of BLM lands.) The National Park Service has two small compensation programs related to public schooling of park employees' children at two parks. PILT provides some compensation for most federal lands, but many lands—inactive military bases, Indian trust lands, and certain wildlife refuge lands, for example—are excluded, and the national forests and O&C lands get PILT payments in addition to other compensation. In 1992, the Office of Technology Assessment recommended "fair and consistent compensation for the tax exempt status of national forest lands and activities."[35] This concept of fair and consistent compensation could be extended to all tax-exempt federal lands. Others argue that the limited costs imposed on local governments by federal land ownership may lead to overcompensating state and local governments.

Basis for Compensation

The legislative histories of the agriculture appropriations acts establishing the FS payments to states (the last of which, enacted on May 23, 1908, made the payments permanent) indicate that the intent was to substitute receipt-sharing for local property taxation, but no rationale was discussed for the level chosen (10% in 1906 and 1907; 25% since). Similarly, the rationale was not clearly explained or discussed for the Reagan tax-equivalency proposal, for the spotted owl payments (a declining percent of the historical average), or for the legislation debated and enacted by the 106th Congress (generally the average of the three highest payments during a specified historical period). The proposals' intents were generally to reduce (Reagan Administration) or increase (more recently) the payments.

The geographic basis is also a potential problem for FS payments. FS 25% payments are made to the states, but are calculated for each county with land in each national forest.[36] Depending on the formula used—the average of selected historical payments from each national forest or to each county or each state—the calculations could result in different levels of payments in states with multiple national forests.[37] (This is not an issue for O&C lands, because the O&C payments are made directly to the counties.)

Source of Funds

As noted above, the FS 25% payments are permanently appropriated from agency receipts, and were established prior to federal income taxes and substantial federal oil and gas royalties. Most of the proposals for change also would establish mandatory payments; lacking a specified funding source, mandatory spending would come from the General Treasury. SRS directed payments first from receipts, then from the General Treasury. **Figure 3** shows the breakdown of FS SRS funding between receipts and the General Treasury. Critics are concerned that retaining the linkage between agency receipts (e.g., from timber sales) and county payments (albeit less directly than for the 25% payments) still encourages counties to support timber sales over other FS uses.

Authorized and Required Uses of the Payments

The FS 25% payments can be spent only on roads and schools in the counties where the national forests are located. State law dictates which road and school programs are financed with the payments, and the state laws differ widely, generally ranging from 30% to 100% for school

---

[35] U.S. Congress, Office of Technology Assessment, *Forest Service Planning: Accommodating Uses, Producing Outputs, and Sustaining Ecosystems*, OTA-F-505 (Washington: GPO, February 1992), p. 8.

[36] There was no discussion in the legislative history of why the payments were made to the states, and not directly to the counties.

[37] The complexity of this situation is shown using Arizona as an example in out-of-print CRS Report RL30480, *Forest Service Revenue-Sharing Payments: Legislative Issues* (available from the author).

---

programs, with a few states providing substantial local discretion on the split. The O&C payments are available for any local governmental purpose.

Figure 3. Source and Distribution of FS Payments

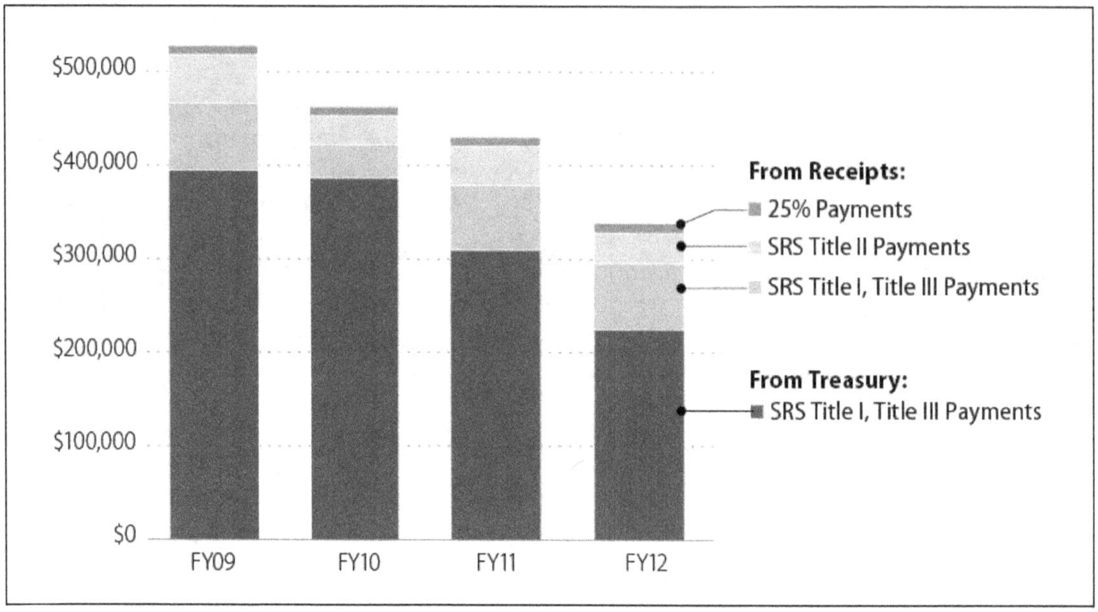

Source: CRS. Data from Forest Service, *FY2010-FY2013 Budget Justifications*, available from http://www.fs.fed.us/aboutus/budget/.

Notes: SRS Title I and Title III payments are passed through the state to the counties to use for specified purposes. SRS Title II payments are retained by the Forest Service for use on approved National Forest projects.

SRS modified these provisions by requiring (for counties with at least $100,000 in annual payments) that 15%-20% of the payments be used for other specified purposes: certain local governmental costs (in Title III); federal land projects recommended by local advisory committees and approved by the Secretary (under Title II); or federal land projects as determined by the Secretary (under §402). Use of the funds for federal land projects has been touted as "reinvesting" agency receipts in federal land management, but opponents argue that this "re-links" county benefits with agency receipt-generating activities and reduces funding for local schools and roads. The Forest Counties Payments Committee recommended granting local governments more flexibility in their use of the payments. The committee also recommended that the federal government prohibit the states from adjusting their education funding allocations because of the FS payments.[38]

Duration of the Programs

The questions Congress may consider are (1) how often should Congress review the payment systems (these or all county compensation programs, or the lack thereof) to assess whether they still function as intended; and (2) what options are available (e.g., a sunset provision) to induce future Congresses to undertake such a review? The FS 25% payments and the O&C payments are

---

[38] Some states include FS payments allocated for education in their calculations allocating state education funds to the counties.

permanently authorized. The FS 25% payments were established in 1908 (after having been enacted as a one-year program in 1906 and again in 1907). The O&C payments were established in 1937. The owl payments were to be a 10-year program, enacted in 1993. SRS was originally enacted as a six-year program that expired on September 30, 2006, but was extended an additional six years through September 30, 2012. The Forest Counties Payments Committee recommended a permanent change based on SRS, with some adjustments.

Appendix. SRS Payments in FY2006 and FY2009

As described in the text, under "Four-Year Extension Enacted in the 110th Congress," the SRS payment formula was modified in the extension to include federal acreage and relative income in each county, as well as transition payments in some states. The result was a change in the payments and the allocation of total payments in the modified formula. These changes are shown in **Table 2**. Note, however, that the change in the payment formula led some counties that had chosen 25% payments for FY2006 to opt for SRS payments for FY2009, and vice versa. Some of the increase in SRS payments in FY2009 is due to more counties opting for SRS payments in some states, such as Michigan, New Hampshire, Ohio, Puerto Rico, and Wisconsin. In at least one state—Pennsylvania—a portion of the decline is due to some counties opting for 25% payments in FY2009.

Table A-1. FY2006 and FY2009 FS and O&C Payments Under SRS, by State

(in thousands of dollars and percent of total SRS funding for all of U.S.)

	FY2006		FY2009			FY2006		FY2009	
	Dollars	Percent	Dollars	Percent		Dollars	Percent	Dollars	Percent
AL	2,133.8	0.44%	2,236.2	0.44%	NY	16.9	<0.01%	29.5	0.01%
AK	9,377.2	1.92%	18,760.5	3.68%	NC	1,020.9	0.21%	2,326.6	0.46%
AZ	7,289.8	1.50%	16,688.2	3.27%	ND	0.0	0.00%	0.8	<0.01%
AR	6,568.0	1.35%	8,309.6	1.63%	OH	68.8	0.01%	339.7	0.07%
CA	65,279.3	13.44%	50,125.6	9.83%	OK	1,238.9	0.26%	1,192.4	0.23%
CO	6,338.7	1.31%	14,641.3	2.87%	OR-FS	*149,153.3*	*30.72%*	*121,316.4*	*23.80%*
FL	2,504.5	0.52%	2,862.3	0.56%	OR-O&C	*108,852.0*	*22.42%*	*87,175.0*	*17.10%*
GA	1,304.6	0.27%	1,864.1	0.37%	OR-Total	258,005.3	53.13%	208,491.4	40.91%
ID	21,173.5	4.36%	34,900.0	6.85%	PA	6,491.6	1.34%	2,505.6	0.49%
IL	304.2	0.06%	107.6	0.02%	PR	0.0	0.00%	184.7	0.04%
IN	130.2	0.03%	337.4	0.07%	SC	3,288.2	0.68%	2,498.4	0.49%
KY	682.1	0.14%	2,596.9	0.51%	SD	3,823.4	0.79%	2,931.1	0.58%
LA	3,726.1	0.77%	2,620.1	0.51%	TN	560.3	0.12%	1,428.4	0.28%
ME	41.4	0.01%	99.3	0.02%	TX	4,688.8	0.97%	3,655.9	0.72%
MI	789.8	0.16%	3,397.1	0.67%	UT	1,872.5	0.39%	14,177.0	2.78%
MN	1,468.8	0.36%	3,330.1	0.65%	VT	392.3	0.08%	400.7	0.08%
MS	8,287.2	1.71%	7,705.7	1.51%	VA	925.2	0.19%	2,093.7	0.41%
MO	2,767.2	0.57%	4,681.7	0.92%	WA	42,293.9	8.71%	33,990.9	6.67%
MT	12,934.8	2.66%	24,523.6	4.81%	WV	2,006.3	0.41%	2,356.8	0.46%
NE	55.6	0.01%	584.4	0.11%	WI	577.6	0.12%	2,730.1	0.54%
NV	408.8	0.08%	5,174.2	1.02%	WY	2,387.4	0.49%	4,357.6	0.85%

	FY2006		FY2009			FY2006	FY2009
NH	0.0	0.00%	275.2	0.05%			
NM	2,383.6	0.49%	18,185.9	3.57%	**Total**	**485,567.7**	**509,667.8**

Sources: FS: U.S. Dept. of Agriculture, Forest Service, "All Service Receipts (ASR), Final Payment Summary Report PNF (ASR-10-01)," unpublished reports. **O&C:** U.S. Dept. of the Interior, Bureau of Land Management, *FY2011 Budget Justification,* p. X-6, http://www.doi.gov/budget/2011/data/greenbook/ FY2011_BLM_Greenbook.pdf.

Note: Counties could choose to receive the regular 25% FS payments or 50% O&C payments, rather than the SRS payments, and in many cases opted for the 25% in FY2006 or FY2009, and sometimes in both fiscal years. Thus, a change in the SRS payments in the table might not reflect the total change in FS payments to that state.

Author Contact Information

Katie Hoover
Analyst in Natural Resources Policy
khoover@crs.loc.gov, 7-9008

Acknowledgments

Ross Gorte, retired CRS Specialist in Natural Resources Policy, made important contributions to this report.